A FALLING KNIFE HAS NO HANDLE

YESYES BOOKS *Portland*

A FALLING KNIFE HAS NO HANDLE

EMILY O'NEILL

ISBN 978-1-936919-62-8
PRINTED IN THE UNITED STATES OF AMERICA

PUBLISHED BY YESYES BOOKS
1614 NE ALBERTA ST
PORTLAND, OR 97211
YESYESBOOKS.COM

KMA SULLIVAN, PUBLISHER
JOANN BALINGIT, ASSISTANT EDITOR
STEVIE EDWARDS, SENIOR EDITOR, BOOK DEVELOPMENT
ALBAN FISCHER, GRAPHIC DESIGNER
COLE HILDEBRAND, SENIOR EDITOR OF OPERATIONS
JILL KOLONGOWSKI, MANAGING EDITOR
BEYZA OZER, EDITOR, SOCIAL MEDIA
AMBER RAMBHAROSE, EDITOR, ART LIFE & INSTAGRAM
CARLY SCHWEPPE, ASSISTANT EDITOR, VINYL
LEVI TODD, ASSISTANT EDITOR, VINYL
PHILLIP B. WILLIAMS, COEDITOR IN CHIEF, VINYL
AMIE ZIMMERMAN, EVENTS COORDINATOR
HARI ZIYAD, ASSISTANT EDITOR, VINYL

for Daren

MENU

A FALLING KNIFE HAS NO HANDLE

SERVICE NOTES

they call it *soft opening* to unbreak each dropped plate
before it hits the floor / language meant to carry
in reverse / *guests* instead of *customers* so that

I unbecome myself tableside / telling stories of how dressed
in animals I am / how many I've eaten raw / strange
butter of uncooked flesh / I get asked

how many Japanese places have been mine & lying
goes against the culture / I say *none*, that my first home was Chinese
steam buns with P. Tang in Cambridge / glass panel rung

like a gong when guests walked into smoke / Phil the pickle
genius / Phil's sriracha cashews & braised beef cheeks / his rice
noodles like fat blind grubs from my grandfather's garden

Phil in the basement prepping to metal when I'd run down
to get the day's bin of beer / Blayne's clipped laugh
at the window / Junot kissing both my cheeks when he found out

we're both from Jersey / I say my new restaurant's old name
& it's a rubbled temple / tiny & full for years before
we ousted the floor manager sweating through every shift

behind our storage shed / before I came home this room was called
the Hong Kong & flooded with drug stories / before the livers
gave me my death week bad as bad oysters / before sawdust

was swept away before / I came in red lipstick
my hair, seafoam cloud for my interview / before
Chef told me *this is our culinary hamster wheel*

service, a dance of clawing forward without leaving
where you begin / more charcoal on the fire
so many mouths arriving, unfull

IT'S TOO DANGEROUS TO TELL THE TRUTH ALL AT ONCE

people begin with *this poem is*
& I want to interrupt them
to admit unvarnished

to lick sugar
from your fingertip / to attempt
knowing the rate of failure

how many parking tickets is it worth
to risk saying what you mean & being
heard? I tell the Dad story

where he meets Capote at a bar
& they both stare at some redhead / a cipher
for hunger with no outlet

because even though she dies at the end
she was loved enough / Pacino robbed a bank
over it & that movie cracked a year in half

you know Dad is dead by now & so is Capote
& the friend who bought their drinks & the bar too
but you're still listening / so it's not maudlin

worth mentioning if it pairs
with what else is on offer / me, touching your hand
when I make your change / parking meter running out

THE POSSIBILITY OF HAPPINESS

can we pretend February makes sense
or that bleeding is enough / to sew me back together
scabby knees as in / the best version

of myself when I still ran / no problem
yes I have guns now yes I'm a bitch
locking up for the night / pulling down the metal gate

& a grand a week to teach people / what to want
when I was seven I told my dad I'd marry
Indiana Jones because / he has a whip

I'm proud to scream your name / when I need you
proud of that sound & the one a shot glass makes
when it meets the table, empty / power comes

from exploiting what's possible / I'm happy with my body
in the right dress & the truth written
on my eyelids / some secrets just pretend

they're the best part / we're the kind of men
who only react to knives but I'm no man
at all / my jaw, too fragile, wiring itself shut

PREPARING MY OWN DEATH

sometimes depression is the bathtub
full & boiling / the book about Florida
leather seats where boys are taken

away from themselves / about remembering
only what you're forced to: I don't know why
I told you I'd kill you in the street

I threw up oysters for 2 days as punishment
for dragging you down to touch the ocean instead of kissing
strawberry seeds out of my own teeth

it's hard to eat knowing where I've been
I can't stop me from horsehide / can't suntan
the virgin out / I'm shy & nobody believes me

it took three years of seeing you daily to admit
I haven't been to any country but this one
there are programs written to force chance

encounters but I'd rather someone
familiar on a whim
towards dissection

I'd rather your logical hands
on a metal spoon / unclouded ice
losing my edge / dying doesn't seem scary

when death is poured for me: tallish glass
of sherry or that light mushroomy wine
color of antique lace / I walk past

perfect windows at La Perla
on my way to teach & the fur
around one mannequin's shoulders

is enough / I give up / it was an accident
I didn't plan on a blood & sand
but I do always want more

more scotch / more flame / more raw / more
want to wear because I'm thinner
than when we met / blinded by hunger

I make noise & call that safety / buck
the bed two feet from the wall
the memorized proof: what's loud

can't call itself afraid / what's afraid
can't cry out when startled / knife / tear / orange
oil hurling match across a glass mouth

if I die I'm prepared to pour down a drain
mixed with sweat & whatever else
made me / where is your mind now?

somewhere outside
the body? don't make me explain
why my mouth remembers

they drink it sugar, lime, simple
in Martinique but here
we luge cognac through the marrow

there's a strong difference
between Hawthorne & julep strainers
it's about escape

they take the menu away
& it's you / your fault
you know too much

THE COOKING HYPOTHESIS

we are supposedly the only animals
applying heat to our food / to enhance it / but
dogs bury meat for fermentation & birds know

how to sprout seeds / so when you ask about Boston
burying his bones / what it means / how he knows
to save what's precious (marrow, or a gift)

we could blame bubbles every night since
Christmas / how we marry places as we grind them down
between our cheeks / I get anxious mentioning

how I cooked today / if it tasted remarkable / it can't
when I'm only dull knives & no practice / a bird
bringing seed to water / hoping I get to eat

soon, the White City / what flying
together would taste like / whole world teasing
my walnut drunk / my thimble

glass / my missing what I hope we leaven into / flavor
of where food was made found in its preparation / buffalo
mozzarella imported / directly to our strange table

tomato sandwiches from my childhood garden / red steaks
still sun warm / melting in wheat toast & the future—my solarium
full of herbs / you, buying me pyramid salt

a fireplace / range big as my body sprawled
across a fitted sheet / what perfect kitchen is there
what fills the pantry / when will we go

IT BELONGS IN A MUSEUM

Paul Revere's punch bowl removed / replaced
by an expensive replica / the whole wing smells of shortbread
& we kiss / Thomas Jefferson glares & wine offerings

are cheap & sharp & wrong for the room / most people
here, parading their taste violently / drinks should exist
with the same forceful perfection / of a tongue

caked in gold leaf / you cringe & say
you don't like it / I cry a little when
the docent says the mailman's touring Europe

I want the warmth of holding marrow
you would recognize / still
inside a body / the frothing horses

Nature revealing herself before science / her eyes
snake-slit in brass / we see a leg shackled
in sea foam / we buy a membership, are asked

if we have the same last name
& we don't / but find the question less alarming
than it could've been / couples visiting museums

must seem married / must hold each other
in the eyes of God, or George
Washington / immediately beside a horse's ass

it's funny / the bubbles sank into my turning
elbow / I hiccup / step forward into the next room
to my favorite painting, absent

one where I found a woman eaten / canvas
stolen off to be restored / & the beads gone too
as if the building shifted / as if you made it new

IF I LEFT A NOTE IN THE MORNING IT WOULD READ

I carry keys to half a dozen houses / but no memory
of the walk to yours / oak leaves hissing
under my boots / I've kept the roses

carved from grapefruit rinds
no one makes me anything but you
this, some accidental guilt admission

a quail's egg, no lipstick sticking to you
or your glass / my mouth a proud trick I play
by saying *always* / what can I offer that might taste new?

when I was wrapping your breakfast
in wax paper I was supposed to be
loving someone else

IN THE TIN, BETRAYERS
(I CALL THEM FISH)

pack them in water / bottle-
nosed in the nets I am / killing
what excess I drown in

glut of used / to loves used to
ladle / clarified butter & call
its fat moonlight / I'm laughing

like I do / at the mattress store
where the seller talks around
my ass / as a problem for sleep

the pressure map / what heat gets
wicked / do we need pillows / frame
& warranty / no one here but us

sees the outline of what still
hooks into my bed / disconnect
at the stomach / how you float

face down / asleep / a raft
I sit on whichever side
& blot out the sea

at home / I sift through
what past is too fixed
to burn / tin of strangers

I once held / thrashing
in my hands / when dragging
a knife / tail to head / the scales

fly as light / to the floor / I loved
them / they spoiled / memory
sealed / key cutting tape

I counted / the whole shoal / a school
of what shone / packed in water
dissolving the bones

ARE YOU IN THE WEEDS

my scalp stained blue
my muumuu / my nonsense
affectations leftover from hippie school

thought I couldn't survive sustained rage
can't build a drink from the dregs / of this
my stained blue neck an egret bruise

my banshee sisters, my brother / a lion
or a bleeding hand so why
when I cry into your shoulder does

my family sound / like trash
I bake potatoes twice & they taste
like your mother is still / alive & full of salt

our inherited deaths / the distance between
us & everyone else / the angle of how I fell
into step with you at all / rude fate

pennies bluing in a pocket / remembering
my dad's Parliaments / hidden behind manila folders
the sherry we drink for your mom

who I will never meet
woman I love because of how close
you still / hold her

& you don't ask me to forget / my blue-edged mouth
in the morning when I've drowned
trying to find my dad

I remember the mountain I stood on
fire tower where / I could see
the world's ending—death winding

towards my father
on the ground / a hawk
whose scream had vital teeth

are you in the weeds / is there only
tall grass now / do you sometimes hate what
hurt I remind you of / am I too many tickets

too few spoons / dry curaçao & orgeat
married until the whole world is Mai tai & mouth
begging less sweet less / sweet please

my tongue shrivels down my throat
thinking how many cherry / seasons I've missed
staring into other eyes / every time I say

I'll meet you at your house I stop / myself
from saying *I'll meet you at home*
because I mean I'll meet you / at you

I mean it isn't weird / to buy a steak
or grind a new key / or invite me to stay
until we leave the place to someone else

THE ROPE IS JUST FOR DECORATION

I'm rude / a child using the wrong fork
forgetting my napkin / I went away that first sip
to a couch in a stranger's basement

tasted Becky's lip ring & a decade
afterwards / I spend too long wondering
if a split bottle of wine means

people are fucking / but it's not something you ask
the first place we stop for dinner is doomed
& wooden / we don't talk except about the cab radio

tuned to Paterson's perennial comeback kid—
Fetty Wap is an ass man / probably fell for the same scene you did
Catherine Zeta-Jones sliding arched under gridded lasers

recognizable desire / common as brown bread
except when you don't recognize want at all
find it disguised in garlic / lamb neck too gamey

a dearth of salt / missed appointment / you bubble
like a fish tank & I've forgotten
Ted's name & where we met / again

often I pass as one of the boys
by acting crass / saying *yes*
then eyebrows raised dramatically

why drunk straight girls
take my hand / demanding we leave best friends
the pick up time is criminally quick

I cry all the time about organs
grown on the backs of rats or stem cell mapping after
we've already lost what we're going to

sipping past then press rewind
to seethe & ask one more time / am I
nothing like I used to be

YOU DRINK WITH YOUR EYES FIRST

when the color makes
your molars ache or the roses
come too late & are left

behind for the cleaning crew when
you would have Tank 7s at my bar
the summer I wore the same boots

no matter the heat / black leather
stacked heel & Levi's cut-offs
rude as every photo I haven't sent yet

I was leaving him & free to swan
dive or better still belly flop into French 75s
mid afternoon & Kentucky Trevor promised

me a bicycle & that he'd be back to see
whose horse finished first
& I can't stand not knowing

if I knocked into your elbow
with an empty tray / or why I got engaged
a 2nd time just after I got laid off

but before you were a regular
at the bar where the syrups poured
like almost-amber & I wasn't good at pretending

I didn't want to go home with you again
which is why we'd stand just beyond the door
talking & I'd smoke before 3 which I never do

because you made me nervous & you knew
about it didn't you? couldn't you always
read the heat passing through me in waves?

RESEARCH & DEVELOPMENT

I can't filet without some casualty
tell me how to tie knots / how to stoke
or slake a campfire / a soreness / a letting in the shoulders

there must be a book to teach bleeding
remember leeches / paintings of medical theater
how the body gets dismantled

or performed / while you're out of town
I'm sleeping in your bed / where we've done nothing
wrong & still I feel guilty

for keeping keys or closing my eyes
a letting of blamelessness / a whodunit gathering
like rain in my cupped palms / my ankles clicking

there's healing in what's discovered
your want, a kind of medicine
for absence / some bottles are marked poison

if I could hold you in the reading
room / if we followed rules there might be certainty
in adherence / there might be time to rest

it isn't important where
I shelve myself / I'm always returned
to where I'm unreachable

DARLING, I WANT YOU BUT NOT SO FAST

I got too lonely & cooked for two by mistake
come over / I'm making Godfathers
there's flourless cake to drown in

I've changed my mind / I don't want to be
this easy / have you ever fallen
in love / with a way out? as a lover

escape leaves nothing / to be desired she changes
clothes three times a day / smells like peat & salt
skin & I got too lonely to stay the same

strip the bed & dress the room redder / no staining
what's already bled / I'm saying I'll confirm nothing
on the grounds I may incriminate myself

I want to use a blade to unlock a joint / to be a man
& carve dinner apart as if I've ever killed & continued
down a path / the ending a trailing hem

I taught myself piano once, played all night
then promptly forgot how to spread my hands
everything is fine / I can't close the door

if I do the deadbolt won't slide / I'm telling you this
in case of unexpected urgency / in case
you call me back

OLD FASHIONED

I bought a bottle of rye tonight / some dark
salted chocolate, a plate of linguini / a seat
for three hours after hearing you sigh from Chicago

little lemon tongue floating / could I ever impress you
when you are a perfect last name / when you know
everyone sitting & every rotten part of me

make the bed with us in it always / furnace / you make
me furious / porter risotto at two in the morning / sherry
vinegar / peanut butter / my hand hooked

under your left ear or / what you called the worst part
& the most comforting thing of all / sorting
herb leaves / propping up a thought / could I arrive

in time to catch your suitcases / the correct garnish for
an unexpected delay / as if I've known
for years how to carry this

a letter delivered by hand / copper

patina / conducting me towards the wrong sleep

ungated flight / unabated sweetness here

the ice is not enough / I know to pour

too generously / I know

it's only one or two more days

this waiting / I know how

I am greedy / what work

starving takes

BROKE (ALONE) AT AMATEUR HOUR

I let a man buy me a drink
tonight & it felt like us / meeting
in reverse / liquid landing

in the wrong hands / how I was
told to call you family / so I trusted
you but guarded my wrists until

we were inside / a snow globe
& you finally fed me something other
than money & *hello* / told me about

the concert with your brother & outside
all those rabbits & swans / Carrie & Lowell
& understanding death / is a meal

to push around the plate / as it cools
I admired how quiet you got
how swagger / didn't sit on your shoulders

is there air enough / for what I have yet to say
that you sleep / pulling your beard
like it might come off in your hand

without the disguise / a new life where
I don't have to hide that / photo
of you & the mojito pitcher in my wallet

an unpaid tab / I told that man to assume
there's an arm around me / even when
it's invisible / I am singing

& you once told me / I scratch my nose
in my sleep like a rabbit / I am so happy
to feel soft again / to not be smacked naked

by what someone else wishes I was / a year
to the day I took the interview that carved me
a figurehead for your afternoons

I am braver for your breath / safe enough
to be angry at intruders in real time / air
enough for a new city inside the bottle

QUEEN'S SHARE

have I told you the one about my therapist
seeing me in a dress for the first time
in 5 years of appointments

on my way to celebrate reviews
with you / the date that couldn't be
we never set our watches correctly

twelve minutes until biscuits & honey butter
in bed / do you understand how desperate I am
to impress / gin / Aperol / holding my glass by the stem

pushing through sober pride
to sing to you / tequila still
in its wooden box / spread so smooth I forget

lime or salt / how many hours did we sing
my head in your lap after Torontos & Cincinnati Hot Brown
sandwiches / I dream we're on a porch swing

in Tennessee / don't want to scare
the safety off / you've shot a .22 & fallen
asleep in Spain / I'm uncultured

licking my fingers clean / reverse
seed of the season / parts of night belong
held to your chest / I'm sorry

for yawning with questions / for only pouring
heads & tails of what's made me this way
for promising to vanish while begging / to stay

NOT BECAUSE YOU HAVE TO

case of lemons passed to me
across the counter while
I swung the gooseneck kettle wide

& watched the grinds wince larger / Colonel
Taylor in a brown medicine bottle / the fernet
your friends brought back from Italy

as a reward for watching their dog / you, pouring
off a sip for me / shaking egg whites
until they mimic latte foam

tiny hearts drawn in bitters / fried pickles
when I wanted to cry but didn't
my hands, brown with morning

I rode my bike because
I had to / called me hiding *mood hair* / as if
every change were voluntary

how many twenty dollar bills
needed breaking / how many times
did I refuse meeting your eye

didn't we first talk when it was snowing
a day you arrived early & I was alone / singing
a city I don't know / you & all your little gifts

begin there: my favorite gray shark cup I can't find
the nose, a memory organ / poked through the surface
of pomegranate tea / coffee matched with thimble daiquiris

bread is really about the air trapped
inside it / the flavor of a time & place
I kept you awake every time you asked

THE RUM ANNIVERSARY

our first bar had a verb for a name
a perfect Lincoln Continental parked in front
& every glass, a face puckered around pellet ice

I hated rum as a rule / from college
where I insisted / ginger ale turned the spice vanilla
I'm not as smart / as a machete

blade falling through cane
unable to cull & process / what's sweet or worth
saving in a single day / me sweating in your kitchen

before rum before I imagined you / too particular
to kiss (hungry) I called it *too much*
overwhelmed that it wasn't whiskey

poured for once & what's a buzz besides
a blurring of intention / I didn't
think you had a house at all

you / too kinetic to live anywhere but in water
rushing past me / so I drank from the sink like a dog
dripped / under my dress, then took it off

it was only May / not the kind of day that boils
unless you stop watching the stove
I walked away until caramel bubbled three times its size

& stained the pot bottom & maybe you're ginger
strung / through my stupid teeth
maybe I need your need

louder than my own breathing
when I say *use your words*
I need to believe you

still in the room / your hands remember me
differently than I deserve / cleaner / less hesitant
silly me / demanding new love / leave the lights on

WITHOUT CONFERRING, WE BOTH ASK FOR A SMOKE & DAGGER

smack me so hard I'm a toothache / enforcing
myself, a victor over savage time / give me
one glass of brut & everything else

give me nothing that might fin you or make this saltier
Gloucester / can you see the harbor
on me anymore / or that savage snifter

size of a lampshade / Shahir sparked
a strike anywhere match & singed
sense to a faint smell / my hair

so long now but still blue / we eat
& eat these animal piles then climb down
into the warmth of it / how much we tartare

how much we pretend no one sees us leave
raise our eyebrows / laugh as though
we've had each other for breakfast more times

than you drink / coffee to wake up / three cups until
you vibrate through the shift, laughing
one clipped shout / tell me to ask for cold brew

tell me Cynar or cider or whatever
fruit you spend on an empty afternoon / just yellow
peppers just Italy / along your lineless forehead

where have I been that you remember / what do you taste
when I round my mouth / kiss, a kind of chef's table
your friends can see me faking / how I always shake

with two hands / a politician / you bite your lip
the Christmas orange / chug from a bottle
of chartreuse / ask who noticed our cab, our hands

our table / full of more plates than we can handle
confidently / I keep the secret by not speaking
the bartender brings bone broth in the most beautiful pot

then pours / the onions
& the chanterelles are still alive
when you swallow

ODE TO HOW I HAPPENED

once a month walk to the deli
for Orange Crush & the pound of mozzarella
I peel apart in layers / eating towards nothing

don't make this a teaching moment / think
about your own head how / your gums leak
when you floss & when you don't

when you open a wall / you're un-bottling bones
tree ribs in there / secrets insulate / blood doesn't
care what it takes to get born

what reflex can I kill? hunger / the throbbing
thought / it kicks / I grit / if there's a recipe
success depends / on the kitchen it lands in

once a month I shredded that wet orb
in my mouth / violin hall of mirrors
the hands pressing me / smooth

rings dropped into the sink / me, cut rhinestone / bones
the only occurrence / territory / the uglier option
my thighs narrowing & this was safety

until / butter on my fingers / approximate maps
wishbone connected to the jawbone
snapped shut / migraine then another harrowing / hunger

no light no heat no / sleeping through
tremor / I wait to swallow a stinger
there's a flower that smells like a carcass

catches flies by dying / causes a flood by opening
this is how it looks inside my head: yarn skein
spinning around stretched fingers / lightning

ribboned fat / what grain & hands
tucking in my lungs / did you see
me & want / a swan?

PRINT TOO SMALL, KITCHEN CLOSED

I am smiling against the overpass
saying the wine will not run out / we ran out
of the lounge & down the alley

dragged by the Aubry / you, so rosy
you kissed me in the street / let them wonder
where the alley led / if we made it home still touching

if trampled violets / not rotting, only compressed
tiny wet flowers from a thin-skinned grape
the tannins whispering / cranberry mustard

brie falling / apart in the room's heat
you don't warn anyone of my name / more important
to fill a mouth with what can be chewed / clean

pink steak & fingerlings / we clean the plate
not carnuba or plastic wax lips / what a difference
a wrapper makes / the wine will not run out

the glass sitting thinner than the color
says it will / let me yell, pen a love letter
regarding / duck poutine & Crown Royal

burnt through with Banana Runts
don't kiss me in public / decant the last sip
don't warn anybody you've had me

POUR TWO FINGERS IN MY GLASS, PLEASE

there's an ad on the train proclaiming *egg health* / I know
I told you I'm broken anyway / when we do the reckless thing
again before breakfast / when you put your arm around me

on the train / I'm not cold / I'm poached / toasted
tasting apples in the Orval / stir up something
red for me / call us equal

the best sound: the torch & pan at 5 AM / the best sound:
why the sky fades paper white / tell me a story
about the bottle's neck widening / why espresso

sticks to my teeth / why you have parking tickets
with my name on them / how the yolk still runs
onto the plate / it feels like a snarl to cross the river backwards

hat tipping down over my eyes
don't see why another hour can't be tithed / to flowers
I won't give back a second time

your house on fire / alarm stinging us
back into our own bodies / I let you cook
when I said I couldn't stand it

every course, a cheese course / let this age properly
see me failing at loneliness / your number called
at the butcher shop / what can I do for you

WHEN I WAIT UP HALF THE NIGHT FOR YOU

you don't call but it can't matter
I've gone off-recipe / thirst
is a cursed word

so I don't say it out loud / ask instead
have I fished today? have I wiped off lipstick
because of what's in the wax?

there's a man raising foie gras geese
without force-feeding them / he lays down
in their field / wings sliding over his jaw

they stay & eat because
he's never built a fence so their livers hold
more lemongrass than fear

the best ham in the world is fed
on acorns & most wild boars are escaped
domestics sharpening their teeth

you invent a game where
a bartender kisses a drinker
then guesses what's in their glass

who am I / tasting Balvenie / dark
chocolate, coconut or dry, sharp junmai
spread on my tongue

I overhear the recipe for your mother's
holiday punch: 2 cups vodka then apricot brandy
a bottle of chardonnay then a bottle of ginger ale

any better than bottom shelf cuts it
am I looking / for a label I recognize
is it weasel or stoat or mink

or a rat that I mean / aren't all low things just
soft cousins / your eyelashes inky matinee idols
people pay plenty to fake

HOW I RUIN EVERYTHING BY
SAYING IT OUT LOUD

I am not feeding myself / to a bad man
but I'm not the one / driving the car
tonight & won't exit seriousness

before the carving station / cannot see myself
boiling until someone scalds / a lunch ruined
by inconsistent stirring / what kind of monster

eats / salted butter from the crescent of a fingernail
why do I pull the edges / until blood comes
I see you not wanting to be seen

I'm sorry for scaring you / bolt upright
in bed / your hair a rooster comb
when I sneak in to steal back books

I want to take a picture where
you aren't cringing / to watch you move
through strings of tiny chives or ramen cacio e pepe

you say my name out loud only to other people
& I can name that hesitation
if I blow it now / the loss will be specific

how a room smells when bread chars
too bitter to salvage / a dish cracking
as it lands hard in a porcelain sink

KITCHEN NOTE: SEVERE SEAFOOD ALLERGY, SEAT 2

at dinner with Nai I ate a fried clam
& when I kissed you hours later
you didn't die / the mouth is sometimes a liar

or scrubbed clean
by liquor / there are rooms
we can't enter / take me to the desert

instead of the beach
mezcal in little clay pots / call it *cactus vodka*
it's a joke, how a menu hides its menace

ask the right questions to be sure
nothing will harm you here / I've stopped risking
sips of shell (your death sentence)

a hard no to tentacles, gills, & sea cockroaches
if I could have anything for dinner
wouldn't I ask you to choose? / more jokes to borrow

more time / I have the same last name as the dead drunk
playwright & Charlie Chaplin's final wife / still no one can spell it
same as everyone interrupting your first name with a second R

we miss meals / switch seats when
shellfish lands at your elbow
concern a kind of fear

consider the oyster the way it was intended
snapped shut around a polished accident
I wash my hands twice / keep my hair pinned back

worry tattoos me with pearls / worry that
you can't touch me without hives
& your throat swelling closed

IF YOU SALVAGE THE SPILL

staring at pebbled yellow / glass you
stole from sideboard fragile / memorial
to the stuffed house / where you gained

height advantage / I wear heels to trip
into you on purpose / excuse to hook
hand around pulse / scared again

of leaving lights on / climbing out of bed
into relentless Tuesday / saffron not a spice
but marigold stamen / pansies soft & edible

sunflower starfish plowing over circular bones
what might you eat / could it be spineless
is there a veal season / did we call it to table

scared again of service ending / before hunger / slaughter
prior to milkman knocking / leaving behind a child / Todd
carving your name into the cabinet / have I told you

fields of plastic Hadley houses / stinking manure
spring / gin a stand-in for water / I lived
a kneeling life / prayer to body stretched

against season / heels sinking into floor
I dwell on what ways we are preserved
children / ruining fairy circles in mushroom forage

no shutter to stop it no skis to step into / no mountain
I could learn to diamond down / without certain fracture
does crystal break for fear of breaking / break my grip

on the glass / little misplaced then rescued
wonder / I trip into your shoulder after dinner
full to spilling / brittle / touched

CATALOG OF LOVES GONE UNDEVOURED

toad in the hole with coffee gravy / panzanella
roasted halloumi / shredded celery root / golden beets
pickled green beans / precise

acidity / vinegar forward / winter root
vegetable latkes & ricotta & my first kumquat
clothbound cheddar grits / maple-glazed pig tails / cheese crostini

to shear sweetness in half / orange wine by the glass
bright & solid / holding myself open
against a window / the sparkle bridge in Fort Point

where we attempt false stars / $100 bottle of bubbles
drunk from a tin boot / *straight to hell*
boys / we've had so many Italian Mondays

magazine loaded / with stewed tomatoes
the ceiling at Capo like the honeycomb floor
in my gram's upstairs bathroom

where I'd banish the mat & press migraine to tile
slow breath / wine, the gun to swallow
willingly / cortado *to shorten* in Spanish

they shovel green peppers into the khee mao
& I get angry when I can't remember the ratios
the way you spout numbers or

quote correct potatoes over the phone
to Pierce & he scoffs / but you memorized
boiled instead of roasted if you're making gnocchi & also

Old Fitz + JK Scrumpy cider = peanut brittle
La Guita + unpasteurized sheep's milk cheese = watermelon
3/4 Ango + 1 1/4 dry curaçao = a better Fireball

texture & taste a careful calculus
women are supposed to have better palates / so you ask
what I've tasted before you'll tell me

not chocolate exactly / but there it is
as the beer mellows / cacao
of course & something greener

IF YOU COULD SEE WHERE I
LEARNED TO COOK

sousing for my gram & I sing her French love songs
I can't translate / she knows it's about eyes & bones & beds
I think / how embarrassing to not speak

the language, to undress parsley of yellow leaves
& crave your tile island / how we don't speak when eating
the coal quiet / sage leaves soft as rabbit

fur / shredded over risotto you are probably eating right now
in Chicago / I had rice for dinner too / from a freezer bag
because she's cooked for three generations

& is too tired for big meals two consecutive nights
I take down the big knife, think
I'm helping & regret / I step outside myself

so quickly / table where my plate would go cold
& wait for me all night until breakfast / each portion
hard & dry & still mine / nothing like

the farro dish we ordered twice / chestnuts
& an open hand waiting to take whatever is left
Gram carving pork into the pan

from the back of the fridge / pulling
paring knife into her thumb again
again / two rabbits in the yard / a hutch

she calls The Rabbit Taj Mahal
we had rabbit meatballs that night, yes?
I keep consistent

enough to eyeball a 1/4 cup of diced onion
exactly / it makes her proud to see me
snapping walnuts down to dust by hand

I'VE BROKEN HEARTS / SLEPT THE SAME

the sorry song follows us / little dubstep nuisance
twisting through the too late / must be dead
as meat drifting off the bone

perfect char & spice / hanging
mid-palate slow spreading heat / stories
you shouldn't hear about harm / thrown

negroni to unlock / what there is to laugh
through / make me soak my feet / make me say
when I've been a watch / when I've closed the oven

on my own hand / what there is to trust in filling & how
long it took me to deserve care / a note
at the top of the ticket / I take over

seeking but the song plays on every station
trying for some slow return / would you believe how he said
he'd be home from Korea / when I said I wasn't waiting

the vinegar is this: I've been
property / stolen / I've walked
off the farm unsupervised / cow, unmilked

heirloom tomato in a pocket / it's too late
to apologize for stealing me back
from a fate / worse than fur in a fridge

wanted but never worn / make me say what new
leaving afforded / dinner for one cooked twice, then
shared with whoever becomes necessary

ALL PILES OF FUR CONTAIN SOME NUMBER OF TEETH

didn't I tell you / the seam ripped
there was a fissure my nose
leaked until / the basement

shelved nothing but flood / rat tides
screamed out into the street Hurley
between 3rd & Sciarappa a sudden ocean

of what steals / food out from under us
my face cracked in half & the sun
coming up so / we go to the only real diner

in Boston / near the hospital I soften into hash
from the flattop & poached eggs / black coffee
to muscle me back to myself / didn't I say

when they tear at me / I can't eat
that my hands end up in my mouth
until they bleed / remember your tongue

so swollen / you couldn't swallow water
I walked the green lined tiles
to find you at the back of the ER

heard them say *there's no medicine*
for this & saw myself in slippers
on a metal bed / the problem

chewing through backs of cabinets
didn't I name fear / the water
as it rises around us both

THERE ARE NO ACCIDENTS

Ryan can't remember the first oxtail
but I know mine was braised / against roots
sweet little string / running past my cheeks

I pour me a little bottom shelf oloroso
& everyone teases me, drunk / my thimble
glass / my missing what you'll leaven into / today

my hair is made of clouds you slept on
I'm beginning to recognize everyone / which makes
leaving Boston next to impossible / the pull to vanish

all but artificial / un-distilled / leave hate to ferment
& it blows bubbles / little triumphant heat / *jamón
ibérico* again / a pig for every person

could you kill one? blame the bottle
how the sigh comes rushing up
against cork / do you need a spoon

or is the bone wide enough for presentation?
is osso bucco / a kind of kissing
how it falls apart when pressed

THE BRAIN IS A HUNGRY ORGAN

& the kitchen fills with smoke
the night you swear / you'd break
Derek's knuckles / for the shadow he left

his error, what sharing a roof smarts of
the broken escalator / pan spitting to sear
dry aged steaks / it's past

the expiration for saying so / for stopping
lock receding into chamber / I sleep
here without careful supervision

I am the wine / tasting of cigars, dark
fruit / bear meat grows up from berries
& people too / we all cluster

around the hot light / call liquid *bright*
when it stings the tongue / call the mind
a trap closing & recognition its trigger

call me sear / shaking against cast
iron / it's midnight & the oven hisses
as witness / I sleep here a cluster

of what tastes / best paired / the bottle
stands breathing / key in my pocket
offering each night on a tray

A FALLING KNIFE HAS NO HANDLE

say it twice / if you can feel wheels
spinning / hard enough to snap an axle
when I clock in I'm sloppy / drop a bottle

back into the speedrack / so fast it shatters
most Mondays we don't work / make time
a new shape / fold it into a hat

buy tickets to standing / still sink into our seats
with spiked Coke Zeros / when I dissolve in the theater
blame my dad / back to life in a Stetson

please say it twice: *we can leave*
if you need to I hold your hand
when the tumbler lands / above her ear

when the bathtub / when bank alarm
when the father says *stardust*
then dies / when I'm filling space

just to let the salt out / you're supposed to
take the blade & say *yes* / to let it fall
without reaching for catastrophe

WHISKEY GOT ME FEELING PRETTY

don't lie about what crystal / you've collected: champagne
bucket, set of sherry glasses / or the kindness you do
letting me rest against your neck / breathing

people say vanilla as if that's a bad thing
but just try mimicking it / or perfect bourbon
ice cream melting into pecan pie / speaking of

perfect / holy trinity of cider, 1972 Calvados, the Old
Fitz bottle descending to the tray table / you weigh me in hand
same as sifting garlic bulbs / in search of what's heavier

than it seems / waiting / make the ending patient
steal the salt / I tell the one about the ski lodge in New Hampshire
door to door Jehovah's witnesses & their kids

stealing the cat named Koala / details so specific
they sound untrue & who could believe us
anyway / waiting at the fence

watching rabbits / where I say *hello, Dad*
& know how strange that lands / but the night he died
there were a dozen rabbits in the street / I swear

I didn't invent the symbol or us
braided & scored & rising / at eleven
every day to mourn morning / missing coffee, missing

palm flat / pulling me warmer / you, your mother's chef
& caution & not the little shit you think
you started as / your twin self

a hiding place / let me forget how to curl my hand
while chopping onion / the soy, the rain, the bastard
halibut / my watch, broken but that clock says

yes / I'm waiting, make the ending / patient / love is
a razor / a bottle aged to savor / four small batch roses & I hope
we pour another jigger / I hope you aren't mad

A WAY OF THANKING THE PIG

so many surprises: I like coconut
now / & you are softest when we lock the door
rabbit fur / or the very best butter

can I call your name without / sounding cross or
should I make up a new one entirely / about how
you sing in such a small voice / unless

it's Dean Martin & we've gotten into the grape juice
again / or how you hold me / in the dark after
days I've felt impossible / like swimming

with Bahamian swine or / how there's a pig
to match each person in Iowa / growing until
it meets the smoker / confession: I tasted new

tartare without you tonight & almost cried
it was too wet / too far from what we want
knocking elbows / when an animal is of utmost importance

say I drank an Ampersand made with Clement Rhum
for dinner / say the man I love quotes Neruda at weddings
but would never write a word willingly

carve my stutter down / into a palatable joke: me asleep
under my coat / feet tucked into your suitcase as it swells
you could take me as luggage to the island

that started / this volley of new preparations
must have been asleep / must have passed out then
panicked thinking / I dozed through your departure

fear mistaken for the primacy of fire / I burn
but I'm not afraid / feel made of the best butter
& I'll confess again / then strike the match

we should all slaughter a pig
at least once / be sure
our stomachs make sense from start to finish

a way of thanking
what we bleed / like Mallmann & his potatoes
or fire pits—there is no half satisfaction

HOW DO I LIVE

I found us a house for less / than crumbs
sticking to the sheets / all I am composed of
this morning, a litany of men

kissing me goodbye on the cheeks & I shake
moonbeams to proper dilution / write
the recipe for our bodies gone

domestic / don't laugh at me for stepping back
from Colin as he sabers the I Clivi
because that name taken to a magnum

of Gaston Chiquet / sent a woman to the ER
& glass still / sits under the skin
astride my orbital bone

not the reminder I wanted
of ironed blue oxfords / of compromise
the flowers coming to me in a cab

like I'm some movie star / I don't want them
or to tell Kevin I live anywhere / but
among bears I live / wax & colored glass

on the backbar / take the plunge he says
& haven't we / already become a ghost
of former longing / this time last year

the letters started / fizzing in me
on the floor at Papercuts & now a narrative
starring / the original hardwoods

a splitting ax / your laugh / the car door
when it wakes me / from waiting / when we are
that fat caged cork / free & flying overhead

YOU CAN'T GO HOME AGAIN UNTIL YOU DO

I guess there's praise / enough left
dormant under wilted ice / hotel match
sulfur on my pulse points

once burnt dragged through
the crease / to line my eyes
I've judged harshly / am a pill

crushed against a book cover
maybe I'm bitter / about being young
enough / to chase sin's shadow

out of the city / I lie to NYU grad students
about relative well-being / fact: KGB
Bar spun me even more Boston / explaining

my favorite oblivion / & a guy who'd sell me
to his family as anyone / but me
I once stripped in the street to dress better

for brunch / threw up midday at Diamond Dogs
& never slept in Astoria afterwards
kissing my own hands / on crosstown buses

& I'm a false tourist when / Giuseppe offers
hot gin, sweet cream, bergamot
& my stomach roil flattens / illogically

I want to hate spring-rotten streets / the rats
& rushing / & not drinking 40s anymore
but there's an alternate thread / in Inwood

with your perfect hands healed
& me running / barefoot towards
the yield sign where we first met

GO COLLECT 1000 SNAILS

the chef of the world's best restaurant says
it's as easy as carrying a basket toward damp trees
though / there's certainly more to eating organs

than / how you harvest nerve bundles / I'm stupid at this
making a roux like Anne would / whisking, not talking
old bread broken apart by hand / broccoli roasting in the oven

add salt to sugar & fat, get an addict / I joke
about not enjoying clams & you're worried
about losing me to what we both love

it's easy to invent that ending / to brown butter
with a unsure hand / let it be plain as comfort food: I won't leave
you for some woman's cooking, can't stop wanting

what I'm wired towards, but I can explain / differently
a little owl reminds me every day / I'm forgetting
my Italian / muddling it with French, Spanish

treating it like wine stuffed into a cardboard box
but who cares how many grapes make it
to my mouth / who cares what I eat

so long as it feeds me
you do your best work / dealing
in acid / homemade ricotta clotting while

I wait for a taste / I promise
every rain-wet shell to you / I'll cook
until you say you've eaten / your share

LOVE IS A WEAKNESS

I love you tortellini en brodo I love you
last glass of Girolamo Russo I love you
Ken & Arthur begging for a raise

they wouldn't give me / all my love
is a weakness / disallowed
front of house / don't sing while

setting the table / or tell Danny Meyer
you only invoke him as patron saint
when it suits the bottom line

I love you birthday / wine room flowers
& the cab they never came in / I love
you crudo cult / I've taken my apron

clogs & flowers / raw to the tunnel on 93
where my love finds me a new job
in minutes / Cambridge liquor license #69

call this letter / from my juicing arm
one of Massimo's shitting pigeons
I am happy to have you / hate me

if it means a set schedule & fair cut
of the night's tips / plus Pechuga when I want it
I love you anchor in the boatless harbor

& me on the far side of the river / where
the VEP's criminally cheap & that reviewer
prick says you over / sauce your pasta

now I'm paid double / plus my love is close at home
cracking / cocktail tins with his blushing hand
making me love most / what I don't have to grieve

RSVP

you can teach it with chopsticks / force a hand
to be both spoon & ice / unmoving / until
properly softened / close the gate / push

forward / pour water how
you'd pour something made
without waste & what a waste

sunlight is on us / our refusals
to stand or speak / it's Monday when starting
means skin when staying means skin when

I binge on supermarket crab cakes / obsess
over the private scandals of strangers while
you're waking up to Rihanna / beard soaked

in catamaran hammock sun / memory of all we taste
passing back through my mouth
as exhaled smoke / I'm quitting

not for you / quitting to improve
my shaky palate but first
another sherry & a cigarette

first of all, I hate sleeping
alone / feel most full
in your hands / difference between

what's done to & for you
why we hate mead or don't ride horse
it's called / abandoning tradition

in Spain they get air in
by throwing their cocktails
from great heights / you do this for me

like the glass will never spill / you hate me
saying *be well* because it comes too easily / hate
what you can't try & when we do the should've dance

each missed meal or kiss curled back so far
it sinks our shoulders / burnt hair / year over year
a tasting / stupid lunch / stupid Tuesday / silly me

doubled at Park Street / telling some woman I'm pregnant
when actually I'm emptying / I'm running
back to bed / a sugared coward

our names on the overpass / don't have to
leave the party when the party is the bottle
we don't finish / I won't let you teach me

the smacked seal / won't get paid
in anger / picked onion hearts
bright as a paper cut

I took all invitations / never
crossed proper threshold
we drink what's fast

now / forget hesitating as a mistake
not a cocktail dying on the mat
call it breathing instead you say

there's no such thing as a bad spirit
& all I see are ghosts / little parties
full of what we didn't do

NOTES

The title of "preparing my own death" refers to the colloquial name of the process for making the national cocktail of Martinique, a ti' punch.

Much of the language around animal food behaviors in "the cooking hypothesis" is heavily indebted to Michael Pollan's documentary series *Cooked*.

The title of "queen's share" refers to the practice of reserving the best barrels of rum produced by a distillery for royalty's special occasions, as well as a limited line of single barrel, single batch rum produced by Privateer in Ipswich, MA.

The full story of the man raising humane foie gras geese in "when I wait up half the night for you" can be found in Act 3 of *This American Life*: Episode 452—Poultry Slam 2011.

"I've broken hearts / slept the same" takes its title from Phoebe Ryan's "Dead."

"whiskey got me feeling pretty" takes its title from Rihanna's "Higher."

Mallmann, as named in "a way of thanking the pig" is Francis Mallmann, a chef whose cuisine focuses on Argentina, especially the fire pit cooking methods native to Patagonia.

The "world's best chef" referred to in "go collect 1000 snails" is Rene Redzepi, chef-owner of Noma, a two Michelin star restaurant in Copenhagen, Denmark. His remarks are paraphrased from an episode of David Chang's PBS cooking show, *Mind of a Chef*.

Massimo and the pigeons referenced in "love is a weakness" come from the episode of the documentary series *Chef's Table*, which begins with Massimo Bottura and his three Michelin star restaurant, Osteria Francescana, in Modena, Italy.

In the same poem, "pechuga" refers to a style of mezcal production where a chicken is hung in the still during the distillation process, enhancing the flavor of the resulting liquor.

ACKNOWLEDGMENTS

Many thanks to the following journals for giving these poems their first homes, sometimes in earlier versions or under alternate titles: *Anthropoid, The Blueshift, Cloud Rodeo, Dreginald, Drunk in a Midnight Choir, Forklift, Ohio, Gramma, Heavy Feather Review, Hot Metal Bridge, Jellyfish, Moon City Press, Palaver, Pinwheel, Rabble Lit, Redivider, SAND, Sidekick Lit, Spork Press, Swarm, |tap|, Vinyl,* and *Yes, Poetry.*

My deepest appreciation for the many drinks, meals, and conversations that facilitated my writing, and very special gratitude extended to the staff (past & present) at the following establishments: Area Four, Attaboy, Audubon, Back Bar, Bar Mezzana, Billy Sunday, BISQ, Blue Hill, Broken Shaker, Capo, Coppa, Covina, Curio Coffee, Drink, East by Northeast, Eastern Standard, Estereo, Fairstead Kitchen, Gramercy Tavern, Green Street, The Hawthorne, Hojoko, jm Curley, Little Donkey, Mamaleh's, No. 9 Park, O Ya, Pammy's, Pegu Club, Spoke, SRV, State Park, The Suffolk Arms, Tokyo Record Bar, Toro, Voltage Coffee & Art, and Yvonne's.

All my heart to the people who've made this book what it is: KMA Sullivan, Alban Fischer, & the rest of my YesYes team, for your dedication to realizing my work not only on the page but as a gorgeous visual object; Sean Patrick Mulroy, for being my ruthless first editor in all efforts; Dylan Black, for trusting me on service bar & welcoming me to a home I'll never truly leave; Anne Warnock, for your example, your heart, & our friendship; Jackie Downey, for making me look & feel like a badass; Maksim Ostrovsky, for letting me teach & helping me learn; Nika & Patrick Orlovsky, for your constant humor, insight, & love, & especially for Fromage. To all my regulars, thank you for your stories, your trust, & for listening, night after night. To all above & the rest of my family, both blood & restaurant—the wine will not run out.

Thank you, Green Street. You make me better by asking me to notice it all & intervene only where I'm most necessary.

Thank you, reader. May these love letters be a celebration for you too.

And Daren—thank you for asking me to the table before I could afford it & insisting what I thought mattered before I had the words. You've given me this world. I hope I've done even a corner of it justice.

EMILY O'NEILL teaches writing & tends bar in Cambridge, MA. Her debut poetry collection, *Pelican*, is the inaugural winner of the YesYes Books Pamet River Prize for women & genderqueer writers, and the winner of the 2016 Devil's Kitchen Reading Series from Southern Illinois University. She is the author of four chapbooks: *Celeris* (2016), *Make a Fist & Tongue the Knuckles* (2016), *You Can't Pick Your Genre* (2016), and *Baby on Bar* (2017). Her recent work has appeared in *Cutbank, the Bennington Review, Jellyfish, Little Fiction, Redivider,* and *Salt Hill. a falling knife has no handle* is her second poetry collection from YesYes Books.

ALSO FROM YESYES BOOKS

FULL-LENGTH COLLECTIONS
i be, but i ain't by Aziza Barnes
The Feeder by Jennifer Jackson Berry
Gutter by Lauren Brazeal
What Runs Over by Kayleb Rae Candrilli
Love the Stranger by Jay Deshpande
Blues Triumphant by Jonterri Gadson
North of Order by Nicholas Gulig
Meet Me Here at Dawn by Sophie Klahr
I Don't Mind If You're Feeling Alone by Thomas Patrick Levy
Sons of Achilles by Nabila Lovelace
Reaper's Milonga by Lucian Mattison
If I Should Say I Have Hope by Lynn Melnick
Landscape with Sex and Violence by Lynn Melnick
GOOD MORNING AMERICA I AM HUNGRY AND ON FIRE
    by jamie mortara
some planet by jamie mortara
Boyishly by Tanya Olson
Pelican by Emily O'Neill
The Youngest Butcher in Illinois by Robert Ostrom

A New Language for Falling Out of Love by Meghan Privitello

I'm So Fine: A List of Famous Men & What I Had On
   by Khadijah Queen

American Barricade by Danniel Schoonebeek

The Anatomist by Taryn Schwilling

Gilt by Raena Shirali

Panic Attack, USA by Nate Slawson

[insert] boy by Danez Smith

Man vs Sky by Corey Zeller

The Bones of Us by J. Bradley
   [Art by Adam Scott Mazer]

CHAPBOOK COLLECTIONS

Vinyl 45s

   After by Fatimah Asghar

   Inside My Electric City by Caylin Capra-Thomas

   Dream with a Glass Chamber by Aricka Foreman

   Pepper Girl by Jonterri Gadson

   Of Darkness and Tumbling by Mónica Gomery

   Bad Star by Rebecca Hazelton

   Makeshift Cathedral by Peter LaBerge

   Still, the Shore by Keith Leonard

   Please Don't Leave Me Scarlett Johansson by Thomas Patrick Levy

   Juned by Jenn Marie Nunes

   A History of Flamboyance by Justin Phillip Reed

   No by Ocean Vuong

   This American Ghost by Michael Wasson

Blue Note Editions

Beastgirl & Other Origin Myths by Elizabeth Acevedo

Kissing Caskets by Mahogany L. Browne

One Above One Below: Positions & Lamentations
by Gala Mukomolova

Companion Series

Inadequate Grave by Brandon Courtney

The Rest of the Body by Jay Deshpande